First World War
and Army of Occupation
War Diary
France, Belgium and Germany

1 INDIAN CAVALRY DIVISION
Divisional Troops
2 Field Troop Sappers and Miners
10 September 1914 - 30 November 1915

WO95/1170/5

The Naval & Military Press Ltd
www.nmarchive.com
Published in association with The National Archives

Published by

The Naval & Military Press Ltd

Unit 10 Ridgewood Industrial Park,

Uckfield, East Sussex,

TN22 5QE England

Tel: +44 (0) 1825 749494

www.naval-military-press.com

www.nmarchive.com

This diary has been reprinted in facsimile from the original. Any imperfections are inevitably reproduced and the quality may fall short of modern type and cartographic standards.

© **Crown Copyright**
Images reproduced by permission of The National Archives, London, England, 2015.

Contents

Document type	Place/Title	Date From	Date To
Heading	WO95/1170/5		
Heading	BEF 1 Ind. Cav Div. Troops 2 Fld Troop S & M Sept 1914-1915 Nov.		
Heading	War Diary of The Field Troop, 1st Indian Cavalry Division Period From 10th September To 31st December 1914 Volume I, pp. 1 to 12		
War Diary	Bangalore	10/09/1914	09/10/1914
War Diary	In Train	10/10/1914	10/10/1914
War Diary	Bombay	11/10/1914	16/10/1914
War Diary	On Voyage	09/11/1914	09/11/1914
War Diary	Marseilles	10/11/1914	10/11/1914
War Diary	Camp St Marcel	10/10/1914	13/11/1914
War Diary	Marseilles To Orleans	14/11/1914	15/11/1914
War Diary	Orleans	16/11/1914	16/11/1914
War Diary	Camp La Source Orleans	17/11/1914	30/11/1914
War Diary	Auchel	01/12/1914	23/12/1914
War Diary	Ham-En-Artois	24/12/1914	26/12/1914
War Diary	St Hilaire-Cottes	27/12/1914	31/12/1914
Heading	War Diary of Field Troop, 1st Indian Cavy. Division From 1-1-1915 To 31-1-1915		
War Diary	St-Hilaire-Cottes	01/01/1915	08/01/1915
War Diary	Gorre	08/01/1915	09/01/1915
War Diary	Festubert	09/01/1915	10/01/1915
War Diary	Gorre	11/01/1915	11/01/1915
Miscellaneous	St Hilaire	12/01/1915	31/01/1915
Heading	War Diary of Field Troop 2nd S & M. 1st Indian Cavalry Division From 1st February 1915 To 28th February 1915		
War Diary	St Hilaire	01/02/1915	25/02/1915
War Diary	St Venant	25/02/1915	28/02/1915
Heading	War Diary of Field Troop 1st Indian Cavalry Division From 1st March 1915 To 31st March 1915		
Heading	St Venant	01/03/1915	11/03/1915
War Diary	Auchel	12/03/1915	14/03/1915
War Diary	Lespesses	15/03/1915	18/03/1915
War Diary	Erny	19/03/1915	19/03/1915
War Diary	St Venant	20/03/1915	31/03/1915
Heading	War Diary of Field Troop 2nd Q.V.O. Sappers And Miners 1st Indian Cavalry Division From 1st April 1915 To 30th April 1915		
War Diary	St Venant	01/04/1915	25/04/1915
War Diary	Ste Marie Capelle	25/04/1915	27/04/1915
War Diary	Watou	28/04/1915	30/04/1915
Heading	War Diary of 2nd Field Troop 2nd K.G.O., Sappers & Miners. From 1st May 1915 To 31st May 1915		
War Diary	Watou (Belgium)	01/05/1915	01/05/1915
War Diary	Ste Marie Capelle	02/05/1915	04/05/1915
War Diary	Roquetoire (Ligne)	05/05/1915	08/05/1915
War Diary	Wittes	09/05/1915	16/05/1915
War Diary	Allouagne	17/05/1915	18/05/1915

War Diary	Wittes	19/05/1915	27/05/1915
War Diary	Staple	27/05/1915	28/05/1915
War Diary	Rubrouck	28/05/1915	28/05/1915
War Diary	Near Ypres	28/05/1915	28/05/1915
War Diary	Near Vlamertinghe H 13 D	29/05/1915	29/05/1915
War Diary	H 13 D	30/05/1915	30/05/1915
War Diary	Near Vlamertinghe	31/05/1915	31/05/1915
Heading	War Diary of Field Troop, 1st Indian Cavalry Division From 1st June 1915 To 30th June 1915		
War Diary	Vlamertinghe	01/06/1915	13/06/1915
War Diary	Hazebrouck	14/06/1915	14/06/1915
War Diary	La Sablonniere	15/06/1915	28/06/1915
War Diary	Rue Du Ponch	29/06/1915	30/06/1915
Heading	War Diary of 2nd Field Troop 2nd Sappers and Miners From 1st August 1915 To 31st August 1915		
War Diary	Bout Delville	01/08/1915	26/08/1915
War Diary	Lacouture	27/08/1915	31/08/1915
Heading	War Diary of Field Troop Sappers And Miners. From 1st September 1915 To 30th September 1915		
War Diary	Lacouture	01/09/1915	30/09/1915
Heading	War Diary of Field Troop Sappers And Miners From 1st October 1915 To 31st October 1915		
War Diary	Lacouture	01/10/1915	02/10/1915
War Diary	Bout Delville	03/10/1915	31/10/1915
Heading	War Diary of Field Troops Sappers And Miners From 1st November 1915 To 30th November 1915		
War Diary	Bout Delville	01/11/1915	07/11/1915
War Diary	Ham-En-Artois	08/11/1915	17/11/1915
War Diary	Mametz	18/11/1915	28/11/1915
War Diary	Senlis	29/11/1915	30/11/1915

No 95/1170/5

BEF

1 IND. CAV DIV. TROOPS

2 FD TROOP S & M

Sept 1914 — 1915 Nov.

WAR DIARY OF THE FIELD TROOP,

1st INDIAN CAVALRY DIVISION.

period,

from 10th September to 31st December 1914.

VOLUME I, pp. 1 to 12.

Army Form C. 2118.

page 1

WAR DIARY
INTELLIGENCE SUMMARY.
(Erase heading not required.)

Instructions regarding War Diaries and Intelligence Summaries are contained in F. S. Regs., Part II, and the Staff Manual respectively. Title pages will be prepared in manuscript.

Hour, Date, Place.	Summary of Events and Information.	Remarks and references to Appendices
10th to 18th September 1914 Bangalore.	No. 2 Field Troop, Sappers & Miners. Summary of events prior to disembarkation at Marseilles. Orders received by the Commandant 2nd "QVO" Sappers & Miners, from Army HQ for the formation of No 2 Fd. Troop strength and composition as in remarks column.* Technical equipment (Army Tables Eng. units Table XIII) to be taken over at Kirkee from 3rd S. & M. to work with the Cavalry Division being sent from India. Capt. E.K. Molesworth (at Rawal Pindi) and the Comdt. "QVO" S&M selected Lieut. T.A. Harris as Troop Comd. & officer, and other ranks equally as far as possible from the Field Companies. Arms and Required equipment requisitioned from Madras Arsenal, F.S. clothing from Local Supply Officer, identity discs, hot rasks, toe plates, &c from Depot concerned. Indents for ammunition requested reference to, and all forms prepared. Letters & telegrams required by mobilization Regns. prepared. D.G.M.W. was requested to sanction purchase of 10 bicycles and ac- cessories. Sanction rec'd next day, and bicycles purchased. F.S. clothing rec'd.	*B.O's 2 NCO's 8 I.O's 2 I.R&F 60 including 10% reinforcement pte 4 2nd pte 6 30% changes 2. R&F to be relieved above personnel to be released from 2nd QVO S&M on Transport. Jongas 30 { to be purchased by (to carry equip QMG's Branch on sup & personnel) plied by HH the 4 T carts 6 Maharajah Scindea Power rations 8 } supplied 2 august 78 } by HH 1 in charge above Transport } The Maha I.O. 1 } rajah R&F 45 } Scindea from JCO'S 11 } I.S. Troops G.S. wagon 1 } to be supplied Cook cart 1 } at Base Water 1 } AT 1 }
19th Sept 1914	Capt E.K. Molesworth arrived from Rawal Pindi, having inspected Tongas presented by HH the Maharajah Scindea at Gwalior en route. Daily instruction in riding for Indian Ranks was begun and continued.	-/- As no scale of regtl. equip* is laid down for a F.T., demands were based on requirements of a F.A. Coy.
20th Sept "	No 2 Field Troop left for Bombay under orders to report all regtl. equipt sent direct Bombay for Madras arrived reported out Bangalore.	
23rd Sept "	Capt E.K. Molesworth and Lt. T.A. Harris allotted a 2nd charger each from the 26th "KGO" Light Cav. Advanced Party of Lt. T.B. Harris and two sergeants left for Kirkee to take

Army Form C. 2118.

page 2

WAR DIARY
INTELLIGENCE SUMMARY.
(Erase heading not required.)

Hour, Date, Place.	Summary of Events and Information.	Remarks and references to Appendices
23rd Sept, 1914 (Cont'd) Bangalore	Over the Technical Equipt from 3rd S. & M., got necessary alterations made, and proceed BOMBAY.	The Advance Party arr'd BOMBAY with the Equipt on Sept 26th, until the arrival of the 3rd Troop on Oct. 11, was occupied in necessary
24th Sept "	Repaired what ready to move from BANGALORE. F.S. Clothing issued to all ranks & followers. Hob nails & toe plates affixed to boots.	Tonga's purchased & fitted in LAHORE, further alterations were carried out by S.&M.T. Rly.
25th Sept "	Drew reserve rations and oil from local Supply Offr. Orders rec'd from Cav. Dn. to be at BOMBAY by Oct 4th.	Some extra equipt. was obtained mainly thro' A.C.R.E. Bombay, and the orders of C.R.E. Cav Dn, including 1st 1600 ft.
30th Sept "	Drew advance of 3 months' pay for Troop & paid out. Orders rec'd from Cav. Dn., Bombay, to stand fast pending further orders.	steel cable, 1st 1600 ft. Electric hang Lamps, Sketch blocks, Pull hooks, Junction bars, Saddlebags 2 oz, Stables & c
2nd October, 1914 "	Orders rec'd from Cav. Dn. to be at BOMBAY 7th Oct. Arranged accordingly with S.S.O., Station Master, and Mule Corps to move 6th by Passenger train.	The ammn. & equipt was taken over from the O.D. at Bombay and the equipt. stamped & marked.
11.35 am 5th October "	Despatched officers' chargers to BOMBAY. Orders rec'd thro' 9th Dvn to postpone move until 8th too late to stop chargers.	
12 noon "		
8 am 8th October "	Loaded up transport. Orders rec'd thro' 9th Dvn to delay departure 24 hours. Entrained all heavy kit etc City Sta.	
4 p.m. 9th October "	Marched off and entrained at City Sta. in ordinary train. Train left BANGALORE.	
6.45 p.m "		
10th October (in Train)	Changed at GUNTAKAL and RAICHUR, where, having arranged for a longer university, 150 men cooked food.	

Army Form C. 2118.

page 3

WAR DIARY
INTELLIGENCE SUMMARY.
(Erase heading not required.)

Instructions regarding War Diaries and Intelligence Summaries are contained in F. S. Regs., Part II, and the Staff Manual respectively. Title pages will be prepared in manuscript.

Hour, Date, Place.	Summary of Events and Information.	Remarks and references to Appendices
5 pm 11th October 1914 BOMBAY	Arrived BOMBAY, met by advance party. Marched direct to ALEXANDRA DOCKS for embarkation on H.T. "BANGALA" (C.8.1.8.10) Major HATE with Gwalior I.S. Transport, having arrived Bombay 8th inst., was already embarking.	* note re sea Ration. The men greatly missed their accustomed meat which was recently eliminated from the sea ration. A small supply of dhall was also arranged for, sufficient for issuing near 2 ozs. per day, as this seems to be essential part of daily food of non Indians, when their vegetables are included in the ration.
12th October	Embarked without incident and put out with eleven other transports at "BANGALA" in a group of 17 troops + 5 AT each lined in convoy sailed.	
5:30 pm 16th October		
16th October to 9th Nov 1914 on voyage	All animals were exercised daily except on one day when too rough. The Sappers did physical training for half an hour every morning, and usually exercise in shifting sand from hold to trimmer, for 2 hours every afternoon. The above kept men & animals very fit. Arrived SUEZ 30th oct., Port Said 31st oct., where Purchased promptly 5 goats for troops.	R.I.M. 3 men sick, sent to Indian sea hospital.
6 am 10th Nov. MARSEILLES	Arrived at MARSEILLES and disembarked. Received Base Orders to the effect that all after arms to be handed to the Ordnance Dept. and changed for later pattern; ammunition '303 to be changed for Mk VII; and pith sun- helmets exchanged also. Also a revised scale of warm clothing to be drawn. Above items carried out at once. The troop then marched to St MARCEL camp, some 6 miles S. E., being the Gwalior Transport of the March to AUBIAGNE.	

Army Form C. 2118.

WAR DIARY
or
INTELLIGENCE SUMMARY.

Page 4

(Erase heading not required.)

Instructions regarding War Diaries and Intelligence Summaries are contained in F. S. Regs., Part II, and the Staff Manual respectively. Title pages will be prepared in manuscript.

Hour, Date, Place.	Summary of Events and Information.	Remarks and references to Appendices
5 pm 10th Nov. Camp St MARCEL	arrived in the dark, having apparently been sent here by mistake, was not expected. Pitched tents on ground heavy with dew. Cne En. Ecadn., HENRI MEYERWERT, attached to the Troop from this date.	yyyy
11th and 12th Nov. do.	stood bus at advance Depôt and supplied kit at the Indian Base Depôt. Left this mn at Indian Base Depôt to form 1st reinforcements with its 3 and at the Indian Base Hospital. Handed all trans kit required to Indian Base Depôt. Orders having been received from the Base Commandant to entrain at 9.5 pm at D'ARENC Station, to Troop of	yyyy
4pm 13th Nov. do	left camp and entrained with to Gadin Transport, run 3 v S. Cav. Fd. Ambulance in the same train.	yyyy
1am 14th Nov. MARSEILLES to ORLEANS.	Started Halt at BEZIERS to the excellent arrangements had been made for men's cothing, curende watering, Latrine etc.	yyyy
6am 15th Nov. do	Halt at CAHORS, where men cooked. Throughout journey, the people most enthusiastic, tea, coffee etc provided at different places.	
5.30 am 16th Nov. ORLEANS	Detrained at Les AUBRAIS (ORLEANS). Intransilient rain. Marched through ORLEANS to Camp LA SOURCE (about 7 miles south). So as time seemed to be in short supply no pitched some tents hewed lying about, and made	

Army Form C. 2118.

Page 5

WAR DIARY
INTELLIGENCE SUMMARY.
(Erase heading not required.)

Hour, Date, Place.	Summary of Events and Information.	Remarks and references to Appendices
17th Nov. Camp to SOURCE Orleans.	To meet camping arrangements. Firstly, the British Officers went in to Orleans to see the Renamed C.R.E., Base office, Camping Dep't officer, and Ordnance Dep't at LA CHAPELLE. A draw reg'd. Through C.R.E. that additional equipment is sanctioned to bring the Field Troop up to new establishment. Prepared indents accordingly.	× axes felling 12 " " hand 8 Hooks bill 16 bin cutters 16 Sych Sandbag 231 Stakes 1 dia Chest 1 Pickets hair Boats collapsible 2 w/roofing w/superstructure Undercarts Tool cart R.E. 1 G.S. wagn 1 1/LUM
18-20 Nov. do.	Employed the men in protecting water supply of camp from frost, which has now set in. Pipes buried in litter of ground found with wisps of straw of thereabts. and kept head of wash with rushes, ditolls, and new wisps with rushes. Cold wave in camp. Physical training. Draw 2 C.S. wagns, 1 Cork wagn and 1 water cart from Hvee Transport Dept., 7 A.S.C. Drivers and 12 horses w/h Time. Draw pay m Stoxe from Field Cashier Paid Troops.	
21st Nov.	Draw half of double Tort cart R.E. out from Le HAVRE.	
22nd Nov.	Train ct work at LES GROUES camp protecting pipe line from frost.	
23rd Nov. 24th Nov.	Draw 12 felling axes, 8 hand axes, 16 wire cutters, 16 hooks bill, 40 sandbags (to bring total to 200).	
25th Nov.	Fall of about 3 ins of snow in early morning; snow followed during the day. Received notice from DAORT Orleans to entrain 2.05 night 26/27th. Elim.	

Army Form C. 2118.

WAR DIARY
INTELLIGENCE SUMMARY.
(Erase heading not required.)

page 6

Hour, Date, Place.	Summary of Events and Information.	Remarks and references to Appendices
25th Nov (Contd.)	Dispatched supplies & details of Gwalior Transport Corps to Nose Transport Depot. Men at work on LA SOURCE pipe line.	* 8 Tongas 13 Quivers (including 2 sick in hospital) 1 Dafadar 5 Jemadars 12 R.D. draught horses 1 riding pony
26th Nov	Men completed work of protecting LA SOURCE pipe line. Lieut Harris proceeded to ORLEANS to arrange details of entrainment.	EUs
Night of Nov 26th 27th	Left ORLEANS by train.	8W
" 28th	Arrived BERGUETTE; detrained, marched to AUCHEL arriving there at 5.30 p.m.: billeted. Some of the transport lost its way. Was found and whole unit concentrated by 2 a.m.	8W 8W
" 29th	Equipment arranged.	8W
" 30th	Troop route marched. Lieut HARRIS taken dangerously ill, was taken to 3rd Cav. Bde Fd. Ambulance	8W

WAR DIARY
or
INTELLIGENCE SUMMARY.

(Erase heading not required.)

Army Form C. 2118.

Page 7

Hour, Date, Place.	Summary of Events and Information.	Remarks and references to Appendices
AUCHEL Dec 1st	Route march. Manufacture of "hair brush" bombs × commenced	× 1 guncotton slab & primer, surrounded by sacking to which steel slugs wired on to a wooden handle. Weight 4 lbs.
" 2nd – 7th	Bombs continued. Some 450 total; 50 distributed to each of 3 brigades; (about ten bombs, weight 2 lbs, experimented with. Spring bomb gun attempted, which failed owing to fracture of spring. Road repairs at Divisional Headquarters château. One Loopholed Sentry Box built for sentry on gate of Divl. Headquarters Chateau	SEL SEL
Dec 7th	Lieut WICKHAM arrived from MARSEILLES, as reinforcement to replace Lieut HARRIS.	SEL

WAR DIARY

INTELLIGENCE SUMMARY.

(Erase heading not required.)

Army Form C. 2118.

Page 8

Hour, Date, Place.	Summary of Events and Information.	Remarks and references to Appendices
AUCHEL (cond) Dec 9th – 18th	Experiments with bombs continued. Sample trenches dug in neighbouring field; wooden loopholes constructed. Collapsible boat & equipment arrived: practised assembling raft, and repacking into boat wagon, against time etc.	* Double tripartite
" 12th	Skin disease suspected amongst Gwalior Imperial Service Transport Corps ponies: 2 ponies isolated.	
" 13th & 14th	Started instructing 1st Ind: Cav Div in simple trenchwork. Sapping. Taken from affected parts. Instruction of brigades continued. Lieut HARRIS' first charger transferred to Ambala Cav Bde.	
" 15th	Orders to move at 1 hour's notice, rec'd at 7am; everything packed ready to move, then orders were cancelled. Skin disease diagnosed to be sarcoptic mange: clipping commenced, & sulphur dressing prepared. Clipping was continued until all ponies were done, i.e. until end of the month, and sulphur dressing rubbed well in two or three times.	* Sulphur, Sod Bicarb, Kerosene, Soap.
" 16th	Lieut HARRIS' servant despatched to Ind: Cav. Base to remain	

Army Form C. 2118.

Page 9

WAR DIARY
INTELLIGENCE SUMMARY.
(Erase heading not required.)

Hour, Date, Place.	Summary of Events and Information.	Remarks and references to Appendices
AUCHEL (cont)		
Dec 17th	there until Lieut H's return to the front. 2 W chargers size not despatched on account of lameness of the horses.	
" 18th	Lieut HARRIS transferred from Fd. Amb. to LILLERS, and entrained next day for BOULOGNE, en route for ENGLAND	
" 19th	Orders recd to move at short notice.	
" 20th	One draught horse suspected of mange; isolated. 20 ponies were treated with nicotine, to kill the mange parasite. 3 were accidentally given an overdose, and 3 died from the effects of the poison. Injections of strychnine saved the other 3. These 3 & 14 others all suffering from mange were entrained at LILLERS for ABBÉVILLE, with 7 drivers.	
" 21st	Ordered to arrange night posts to watch for spies, suspected of throwing up rocket signals. Two posts placed, one on a mine shaft, one on a mine stack, so as to cover all the ground round AUCHEL. Lights were seen	

WAR DIARY
INTELLIGENCE SUMMARY.
(Erase heading not required.)

Army Form C. 2118.

Page 10

Hour, Date, Place.	Summary of Events and Information.	Remarks and references to Appendices
AUCHEL (con't)	in the direction of LOZINGHEM. Capt MOLESWORTH, Lieut WICKHAM, and a small party proceeded to try to locate these lights. After a tedious walk for several miles, a "Pavillon" was reached in the middle of the wood PONT DE REVEILLON near ALLOUAGNE, which appeared to be a very suitable place for such operations, but nothing suspicious was found. Departing Mr. Ind. Cav. Div. was consulted in the latter part of two hunt. To bed at 2.15 a.m.	gas
Dec 22nd	Orders at 5.30 a.m. to move at once, followed by orders to move at 10 a.m. Left AUCHEL at 10 a.m. in front. Stores for new billets at HAM-EN-ARTOIS, where the unit arrd. at 4 p.m. One draught horse with laminitis left at AUCHEL; also kollapsible boat & stores for which there was no transport. One lame pony dropped at FERFAY en route; one A.T. cart broke a curricle bar, was left for the night at AMETTES. Lieut WICKHAM retrieved pony & A.T. cart from FERFAY and	

Army Form C. 2118.

Page 11

WAR DIARY
INTELLIGENCE SUMMARY.
(Erase heading not required.)

Instructions regarding War Diaries and Intelligence Summaries are contained in F. S. Regs., Part II, and the Staff Manual respectively. Title pages will be prepared in manuscript.

Hour, Date, Place.	Summary of Events and Information.	Remarks and references to Appendices
HAM-EN-ARTOIS Dec 24th	AMETTES respecting sending billets. Exercise route march: 7 Gwalior drivers returned from ABBÉVILLE. Lieut WICKHAM in motor lorry to BÉTHUNE with 460 hair brush bombs (4lb), returned with 3 sample bombs for hair brush pattern 3lb, one C.I. pipe pattern; also 50 empty cyl. bombs for howitzer. Orders rec'd to move at short notice.	
" 25th Xmas Day	Orders rec'd to move at 1 p.m. Advd party proceeded to find billets. Unit arrived 3 p.m. at ST HILAIRE-COTTES got into billets. Their Majesties' Xmas cards distributed. During the night 2 draught horses fell through a hole into the cellar of the house in which they were billeted. They remained there all night, as nothing could be done.	
" 26th	Dug a ramp out of the cellar & walked the horses out. Badly damaged at all. Scraping taken from draught horses, and orders given to clip.	

WAR DIARY

INTELLIGENCE SUMMARY.

(Erase heading not required.)

Army Form C. 2118.

Page 12

Hour, Date, Place.	Summary of Events and Information.	Remarks and references to Appendices
ST HILAIRE-COTTES		
Dec 27th	Bricklayers rebuilt wall of cellar; clipping & feeding.	
" 28th - 31st	All ponies & horses now out in the open in a field &c. Workshops; repairing tongas, new pole constructed; clipping draught horses & ponies. Troop horses dressings daily. Draught horses disposed to have sarcoptic mange, a separate outbreak to that of the Gwalior ponies &c.	× Gwalior ponies "sarcoptic" Shire horses "sarcoptic"
" 29th.	Princess Mary's Xmas Gifts distributed. &c.	
" 30th.	Horse lines changes to another field on account of excess of mud.	
" 31st.	Capt. MOLESWORTH accidentally killed at about 4.15 p.m. Arrangements made same evening for funeral next day.	[signature] Capt RA ?? O.C. Field Troop 1st Indian Cav. Div.

121/4401

WAR DIARY
of
Field Troops, 1st Indian Cavy. Division

From 1-1-1916   To 31-1-1916

WAR DIARY

INTELLIGENCE SUMMARY.

Field Troop 1st Ind. Cav. Div. Page 13

Hour, Date, Place.	Summary of Events and Information.	Remarks and references to Appendices
ST-HILAIRE-COTTES 1915. January 1st.	Capt E.K. Molesworth R.E. 2nd Q.V.O. Sappers and Miners, was buried with military honours, in the cemetery of the Church of ST HILAIRE-COTTES at 3.10 p.m. JCJ	
" 2nd & 3rd	Workshops: Sample trenches were begun - JCJ	
" 4th	Arranged that classes should be held for the purpose of instructing Cavalry officers of the division in the construction and use of hand bombs of various patterns, and in throwing, lighting and throwing them. Dummy and live bombs made up, trenches for above work dug. JCJ	
" 5th, 6th, 7th, 8th	Bomb throwing classes: Sappers rigging machine gun emplacements, shelters. 100 Cwt iron spherical bombs, & bomb gun arrived.	
" 7th	R.E. Officers of 2nd Cavalry Divisoin attended bomb throwing.	
" 8th	Orders received at 4 p.m. for the troop to move at once to assist SIALKOT Brigade at FESTUBERT. The following details, with a certain quantity of entrenching	

Army Form C. 2118.

Page 14

WAR DIARY
or
INTELLIGENCE SUMMARY.

(Erase heading not required.)

Instructions regarding War Diaries and Intelligence Summaries are contained in F. S. Regs., Part II, and the Staff Manual respectively. Title pages will be prepared in manuscript.

Hour, Date, Place.	Summary of Events and Information.	Remarks and references to Appendices
ST HILAIRE 8th (continued) Jan.y	tools marched off at 6.45 p.m.:— British Officers, Major A.G. Bremner R.E. Field Engineer, Lieut J.C. Wickham R.E. O.C. Troop. Indian Officers 2 British NCO's 1 Indian NCO's & Sappers 30 French Interpreter 1 Gwalior and Indore Imperial Service Transport:— Indian Officer 1 Indian R.& F. 19 Ponies 35 Tongas 4 A.T. Carts 2	
GORRE	Arrived at GORRE at 10.30 p.m. via BÉTHUNE, there O.C. to G.O.C. SIRHIND Brigade. 2 tongas were left for bringing tents and bedding. Reported O.C. Orders received for work on partially-made trenches	
9th		

Army Form C. 2118.

Page 15.

WAR DIARY
INTELLIGENCE SUMMARY.
(Erase heading not required.)

Instructions regarding War Diaries and Intelligence Summaries are contained in F. S. Regs., Part II, and the Staff Manual respectively. Title pages will be prepared in manuscript.

Hour, Date, Place.	Summary of Events and Information.	Remarks and references to Appendices
GORRE 9th (continued) Jany	at LE PLANTIN, South of FESTUBERT. As nightwork only was possible, troops paraded at 5.0 p.m. + proceeded to work. The task was chiefly hurdle wedding to form a breastwork. Some 300 x behind our first line trenches. Work was stopped at 1.15 a.m. 10th as there were no more hurdles. Night was v. dark, with rain, enemy constantly sent up star shell (rockets) immediately after which there was invariable some firing. Bullets mostly all passed high over to working party, though some were low enough to hit Party was sniped at from behind our own lines. No casualties.	
FESTUBERT Jany. 10th	Work as yesterday: firing somewhat less; starshell about the same; and a searchlight for a short time. Ceased work at 12.30 a.m. A broken wagon with 2 horses, driverless, galloped down the road behind the work, coming from the South. Was told that the enemy shelled our ground shortly after we left. No casualties.	yes.

WAR DIARY

INTELLIGENCE SUMMARY.

(Erase heading not required.)

Army Form C. 2118.

Page 16

Hour, Date, Place.	Summary of Events and Information.	Remarks and references to Appendices
GORRE Jan 11th	Returned to billets at ST HILAIRE, arriving at 5.20 pm	
ST HILAIRE Jan 12th	Lieut A.A. CHASE R.E. reported having joined Field Troop: proceeded for temporary duty with Field Troop, 2nd Indn Cav. Divn. Experiments begun with bomb-gun. JCL	
" 13th	Bomb-gun experiments continued: trenches & machine gun emplacements continued. Accident with bomb-gun, a bomb bursting prematurely! no casualties. JCL	
" 14th	Fieldworks continued: bomb-gun experiments continued. London Gazette showing promotions of Lieuts WICKHAM and CHASE to Captain. Capt CHASE returned from temporary duty with the other Field Troop. JCL	
" 15th	Routemarch of whole troop: bomb-gun experiments continued. JCL	
" 16th	Capt CHASE again left for temporary duty with 2nd (British) Field Squadron at HINGES. Loopholing, sapping & communication trenches continued: bomb-gun tests continued. JCL	

Army Form C. 2118.

Page 17

WAR DIARY
INTELLIGENCE SUMMARY.
(Erase heading not required.)

Hour, Date, Place.	Summary of Events and Information.	Remarks and references to Appendices
ST HILAIRE Jan 17th	Workshops and experimental fieldworks continued. 3 spare officers' chargers despatched to railhead, with 2 syces and 1 officer's servant spare.	
" 18th	Cavalry Corps concentrated for inspection. Troop marched out at 9 am, marching off to other billets, that is complete, with the exception of a guard and the Bonlonques. Returned at 3.30 pm. A fall of snow.	
" 19th & 20th	Troop practices in bomb throwing. Workshops, fieldworks.	
" 21st	Fieldworks, workshops, exercised animals.	
" 22nd	Divisional Field Day.	
" 23rd	Machine gun emplacement tested with a gun, alterations decided on; bomb & gun trials.	
" 24th	Reinforcement of 4 Sappers, arrived from Marseilles to replace 4 men sent to Casualty Clearing Station. 2 heavy draught horses arrived.	
" 25th	New machine gun emplacement dug, making up of bombs for O.C. 19th Lancers.	

Army Form C. 2118.

Page 8

WAR DIARY
INTELLIGENCE SUMMARY.
(Erase heading not required.)

Instructions regarding War Diaries and Intelligence Summaries are contained in F. S. Regs., Part II, and the Staff Manual respectively. Title pages will be prepared in manuscript.

Hour, Date, Place.	Summary of Events and Information.	Remarks and references to Appendices
ST HILAIRE		
Jan. 26th	48 hairbrush & 20 jam tin bombs completed Proc. 19 February	
27th	Machinegun emplacement completed	do
	Workshops	do
28th	Practice in bomb throwing; with jam tins & spherical iron	
	Gunpowder bombs. Hand post	do
29th	Workshops; making pickets, H, with iron bands.	
	Orders received at 10.30 p.m. to be ready to move at 2	
	hours notice: packed spare stores at once	do
30th	Still in readiness to move; continued making pickets,	
	2 draught horses, sick, sent to railhead. Hard frost.	do
31st	Still in readiness; continued making pickets; filling in trenches	
	Snow.	do

J.M. Matthew Capt RE
O.C. Field Troop
1st Ind. Cav. Divn

31/1/15

WAR DIARY

2nd Field Troop S. & M. 1st Indian Cavalry Division

From 1st February 1915 to 28th February 1915

Army Form C. 2118.

1st Indian Cavalry Division
Page 4

WAR DIARY of Field Troop

INTELLIGENCE SUMMARY.

(Erase heading not required.)

Instructions regarding War Diaries and Intelligence Summaries are contained in F.S. Regs., Part II, and the Staff Manual respectively. Title pages will be prepared in manuscript.

Hour, Date, Place.	Summary of Events and Information	Remarks and references to Appendices.
ST HILAIRE 1915. Feb 1st	Continued making pickets, filling in trenches &c.	
Feb 2, 3, 4	Making fascines for wagons — orders to be in readiness to move, extended to 5 hours notice. &c.	
5th	Route march. &c.	
6th	Hurdles made for brushwood. All horses & ponies inspected by V.O. in the morning. All A.S.C. personnel, horses & vehicles inspected by O.C. A.S.C. 1st I.C.D. in afternoon. &c.	
7th	Manufacture of hurdles continued &c.	
8th	Sandbag breastwork commenced. &c.	
9th	Orders for field day &c. but subsequently cancelled. General refusing to ride. &c.	
10,11,12,13	Workshops, miscellaneous jobs. &c.	
14th	Very wet — Look motors. &c.	
15th	Hurdle breastwork commenced. Sandbag breastwork continued. &c.	

Army Form C. 2118.
Page 20

WAR DIARY
or
INTELLIGENCE SUMMARY.
(Erase heading not required.)

Hour, Date, Place.	Summary of Events and Information	Remarks and references to Appendices.
ST HILAIRE. Sept 16th 17th 18th	Bricklayers, carpenters, smiths employed at their trades on various jobs — hostile breastwork continued: comparison with sandbag work &c.)	
" 18th	News received that all reinforcements were to join here. Pontil formation of Field Squadrons &c.	
" 19th	Roadmaker experimentally parts; breastwork continued. Visited in evening by G.O.C. Cavalry Corps, who inspected breastwork, horselines & vehicles. &c.	
" 20th	Marched to Canal E. of AIRE. rafted over wagons: banks 5' above waterlevel, making operation of running vehicle on to raft slightly troublesome — Capt. Morin I.A. arrived from Base as reinforcements &c.	
" 21st. Sunday	Restday &c.	
" 22nd	To Canal at AIRE again. — Similar work, but banks lower. Very much easier. Capt Morin proceeds to ST VENANT. &c.	
" 23rd	Workshops: mending broken tailboards &c: packing boats &c.	

Army Form C. 2118.

Page 21

WAR DIARY

INTELLIGENCE SUMMARY.

(Erase heading not required.)

Hour, Date, Place.	Summary of Events and Information	Remarks and references to Appendices.
ST. HILAIRE. 24th Feb 24th	Men at workshops as on 23rd: Self proceeded to LA HAYE, east of ST VENANT & here commenced work by SIALKOT BDE of 1st Div Indian Cavalry Corps on 3rd Line defences between ROBECQ - ST VENANT - HAVERSKERQUE, FORET DE NIEPPE. On return to billets, 3 cases of mumps reported amongst Gurkhas I.S.T.C. &c.—	
" 25th	7.30 a.m. Medical inspection (for mumps) of whole troop — no more cases; certain men isolated — whole troop, less guard, to few G.I.S.T. 4.S.C. marched at 9.30 a.m for LA HAYE, east of ST VENANT: arrived 12.15 (7 mile flye) in work till 3 pm: then marched to billets West of ST VENANT. Onarrival at LA HAYE, during the watering of extra horse, one draught horse (rec'd from remounts some 10 days before) produces a foal, prematurely, stillborn &c.	
ST VENANT		

Army Form C. 2118.

WAR DIARY
or
INTELLIGENCE SUMMARY.
(Erase heading not required.)

Page 22.

Instructions regarding War Diaries and Intelligence Summaries are contained in F. S. Regs., Part II, and the Staff Manual respectively. Title pages will be prepared in manuscript.

Hour, Date, Place.	Summary of Events and Information	Remarks and references to Appendices.
ST VENANT		
Feb 27th	8 am to 4.45 pm employed on 3rd line trench work with Sirhind Bde. 1st M.S. Coy Sprs. — making traverses, revetments; making sod breastwork drawing field; hurdles collected; near LA HAYE.	
" 27th	Sod breastwork continued; another work with expanded metal begun.	
" 28th	Expanded metal revetting completed; sod work continued. All the above period, Capt AH Morris was employed supervising French labour in these defences.	O.C. Field Troop 1st K.G.O. Sap & M. 28/2/15 J.C. Matthew Capt. RE

WAR DIARY

OF

Field Troop, 1st Indian Cavalry Division.

From 1st March 1915 to 31st March 1915

WAR DIARY

INTELLIGENCE SUMMARY.

Page 23

Army Form C. 2118.

Stamp: ADJUTANT GENERAL INDIA — 8. APR 1915 — BASE OFFICE

Hour, Date, Place.	Summary of Events and Information	Remarks and references to Appendices.
ST VENANT March 12th 1915	3rd line trench work continued; revetting trenches	OC
" 2nd	work with RE — (new) LA HAYE, completing earth work, sodding etc. OC	
" 3rd	As above. OC	
" 4th	Bridge to carry continuation of breastwork constructed, and new work started near LES AMUSOIRES at 36th Jacob's Horn. OC	
" 5th	Revetting finished at LES AMUSOIRES, of a small portion further south.	
" 6th	28 reinforcements arrived, via ST HILAIRE. New work commenced new canal, transverse revetting and machine gun emplacement started. Very wet OC	
" 7th	Machine gun emplacement continued, expanded metal revetment finished. Very wet OC	
" 8th	" " finished; draining trenches already constructed. OC	
" 9th	working south from LA HAYE level crossing. Cut made in main channel, & bridged with banks of planks, this to enter reduced water level some 15 inches, thus draining a long line of trenches; general revetting OC	

WAR DIARY
INTELLIGENCE SUMMARY
(Erase heading not required.)

Army Form C. 2118.

Page 24.

Hour, Date, Place.	Summary of Events and Information	Remarks and references to Appendices.
ST VENANT March 10th	Resetting training in trenches still further south towards ROBECQ. Orders received at 5pm. "Troop will proceed to former billets (at ST HILAIRE) tomorrow."	
" 11th	Troop marched to ST HILAIRE. On arrival, rec'd orders that troop should be at AUCHEL before dark same evening. Details left behind at ST HILAIRE packed & troop marched to AUCHEL at 3pm arrival 5.30 pm into close billets. Under orders to move at 1 hour's notice from 5.30 a.m. 12th. OC.	
AUCHEL " 12th & 13th	Troop standing by; including two broken tonga wheels, repairing re-tiring. Difficulty about rations owing to changes from Corps troops ST VENANT to Cavalry again. Telegram having gone astray.	
" 14th	Standing by: animals exercised: men went to bath at a mine. Orders rec'd to proceed to new billeting area, marching at 9.15 pm. to LESPESSES, which was reached at midnight. Horses ponies picketed out, men billeted down by 1.30 am. OC.	
LESPESSES March 15th	Straightening billets: exercise of horses. OC	

Army Form C. 2118.

WAR DIARY
or
INTELLIGENCE SUMMARY.

(Erase heading not required.)

Instructions regarding War Diaries and Intelligence Summaries are contained in F.S. Regs., Part II, and the Staff Manual respectively. Title pages will be prepared in manuscript.

p 22

Hour, Date, Place.	Summary of Events and Information	Remarks and references to Appendices.
16.3.15 LESPESSES	Morning - Exercised men and animals. Afternoon - Tried collapsible boats & found them defective under 2 hour entries	
17.3.15 -ditto-	Exercised men & animals - began fitting & route march under 4 hour entries	
18.3.15 -ditto-	Exercised men - musketry - of animals in draught. Rode to ROBECQ. Bit. Head? went to ENQUIN. Farrier came from Luchens Ambulance & total was on emergent case.	
19.3.15 ERNY	Received orders to join on 18" inst. to proceed to ERNY & following day. Marched to ERNY ST JULIEN 15 kilomes at 9.0 am, via ENQUIN in snow & hail. Polley? brought? made had a "may" body this evening (done)	
20.3.15 ST VENANT	Received orders on 19" to proceed to ST VENANT the following day to carry on with the incomplete defence works. Marched to ST VENANT at 8.30 am 24 kilome etc. arriving at 3 p.m. (12 hrs halt for food). Took up former billets for rank & file - both billets for Officers. Major Brennan & Lt Russell accompanied the Troop	

WAR DIARY
or
INTELLIGENCE SUMMARY.

Army Form C. 2118.

p. 26

(Erase heading not required.)

Instructions regarding War Diaries and Intelligence Summaries are contained in F. S. Regs., Part II, and the Staff Manual respectively. Title pages will be prepared in manuscript.

Hour, Date, Place.	Summary of Events and Information	Remarks and references to Appendices.
21.3.15 ST. VENANT	Troops engaged as previous at support trenches between the 3rd line Defences already constructed. Division into 3 working parties under O.C. Left wing & O.C. Right wing respectively. Pause of 2 am., knock off took at 1 pm. Unemployed draught horses being shown exercised.	App 1/3
22.3.15 ditto	Troops employed in 3 working parties as on 21st	App 2/3
23.3.15 ditto	Troops employed as above. Cavalry working parties around in motor buses to carry on the work traces by Trps. between Villages ROBECQ & ST VENANT, again at former place.	App 3/3
24.3.15 ditto	Troops employed as above at & near ROBECQ - also in tracing redoubt, building M.G. emplacements, revetting breastworks + support trenches.	App 24/3

WAR DIARY
or
INTELLIGENCE SUMMARY.
(Erase heading not required.)

Army Form C. 2118.

p. 27

Hour, Date, Place.	Summary of Events and Information	Remarks and references to Appendices.
25. 3. 15 ST. VENANT	Troop employed as before (8am to 4pm) at roads ROBECQ	Rec 25/3
26. 3. 15 ditto	ditto ditto Six men returned from sick – from Rouen.	Rec 26/3
27. 3. 15 ditto	Troop employed as before. New collapsible boats arrived.	Rec 27/3
28. 3. 15 ditto	Troop employed as before – Sialkot Brigade came to work.	Rec 28/3
29. 3. 15 ditto	Troop employed as before – Sialkot Brigade	Rec 29/3
30. 3. 15 ditto	ditto	Rec 30/3 [signature] Capt
31. 3. 15 ditto	Troop employed as before – Ambala Brigade – Lt. Grosvenor left work to relieve Capt. Stock in charge of civil labour. Tested electrical exploding apparatus.	Apr 3/3

121/5504

Parcel No. 144

mc 6/5

WAR DIARY
OF
Field Troop and O.K.O. Sappers and Miners 1st Indian Cavalry Division

From 12 April 1915 to 30 April 1915

Army Form C. 2118.

WAR DIARY of Field Troop 2nd A.D. S-07
INTELLIGENCE SUMMARY.
1st/1st Cav. Div.

(Erase heading not required.)

Instructions regarding War Diaries and Intelligence Summaries are contained in F. S. Regs., Part II, and the Staff Manual respectively. Title pages will be prepared in manuscript.

Hour, Date, Place.	Summary of Events and Information	Remarks and references to Appendices.
1.4.15 ST VENANT	Still working on defences line between ST VENANT and ROBECQ	
2.4.15 do	Working party from Cavalry Bgde	
3.4.15 do	do Lucknow Brigade	
4.4.15 do	Easter day - holiday - everybody in Church	
5.4.15 do	Received mail - Lucknow Brigade	
6 & 7.4.15 do	Work as before - Meerut Brigade	
9 & 10.4.15 do	do Lahore Brigade	
12.4.15 do	do Secunderabad Brigade	

Army Form C. 2118.

WAR DIARY
or
INTELLIGENCE SUMMARY.
(Erase heading not required.)

Page 29

Hour, Date, Place.	Summary of Events and Information	Remarks and references to Appendices.
13 + 14.4.15	Took on S/gin - Seconded to Boyer	App 1/1.
14 - 16.4.15	do - Sick to Boyer	App 1/1.
17 - 19.4.15	do - Amb to Boyer	App 1/1.
20 - 22.4.15	do Ended on enlistments - Lectures Boyer	App 2/1.
23.4.15	do	App v.
24.4.15	do about noon received orders to Byron Car No 1 to move at once. Started to Cour Base at 11 p.m.	App 2/1.
"	Command of M/T Column of STE. MARIE CAPELLE was HAVRIN CROIX and	
25.4.15	and arrival at STE MARIE CAPELLE at 9.30 a.m. 25th. Ran the night and early morning very cheek did not manage to get the Trans there.	
STE. MARIE CAPELLE	As the Transport Officer (Major) + 9+7 of 7 which form 2 Car closed motor buses we have men's transport + have Brennan + Lt Grnell accompanied Trap.	
26.4.15	Visits + home arthur known	App en.
STE. MARIE CAPELLE		

Army Form C. 2118.

WAR DIARY

INTELLIGENCE SUMMARY.

(Erase heading not required.)

Instructions regarding War Diaries and Intelligence Summaries are contained in F. S. Regs., Part II, and the Staff Manual respectively. Title pages will be prepared in manuscript.

Page 30

Hour, Date, Place.	Summary of Events and Information	Remarks and references to Appendices.
27. 4. 15 STE MARIE CAPPELLE	Standing by, at one hour's notice. During night received intimation that Bde was not wanted that night - but some patrols (some arr.) next morning.	AC/3/11
28. 4. 15 WATOU	Standing by, at one hour notice. At 11 am received orders to proceed to certain point at 12.45 p.m. & proceed to WATOU just over the Belgian frontier on the road to POPERINGHE & YPRES. Marches commenced at 12.10 p.m. and Bde ready to move at 1.45 p.m. arrived at WATOU at 3.20 p.m. with transport. Wagons & horse lines. A section dismounted supper left 'B' Echelon at STEENVOORDE CAPELLE. Came on during night of 28-29.	AC/5/11
29. 4. 15 ditto	Standing by, at ½ hour notice.	AC/6/11
30. 4. 15 ditto	ditto. Small working parts to supper details to mend /save roads for heavy traffic.	AC/7/11 ...

Gulab Singh & Sons, Calcutta—No. 22 Arms C.—5-8-14—1,07,000.

Serial No 1444.

WAR DIARY
OF
2nd Field Troop 2nd K.G.O. Sappers & Miners.

From 1st May 1915. To 31st May 1915.

Army Form C. 2118.

WAR DIARY
INTELLIGENCE SUMMARY.
(Erase heading not required.)

Instructions regarding War Diaries and Intelligence Summaries are contained in F. S. Regs., Part II, and the Staff Manual respectively. Title pages will be prepared in manuscript.

Hour, Date, Place.	Summary of Events and Information	Remarks and references to Appendices.
1. 5. 15 WATOU (Belgium)	Under 1 hours notice. Working party mending road. Left at night received orders relative to STE MARIE CAPELLE next morning at 6. (leading unit)	
2. 5. 15 STE MARIE CAPELLE	Left WATOU at 7.30 am & arrived STE MARIE CAPELLE at 9.45 am. Took up various billets.	
3. 5. 15 do	Under 4 hours notice. Practising firing charges with electric gear.	
4. 5. 15 do	Capt. Wickham & Lt. Greenall visited Cavalry to inspect explosives. Boat practice. Received orders to move same night.	
5. 5. 15 ROQUETOIRE (Ligne)	Left STE MARIE CAPELLE at midnight 4th–5th and arrived ROQUETOIRE (Ligne) at 7.30 am. Thick fog all night. Settling down into billets.	
6. 5. 15 do	Settling down and getting ship-shape.	
7. 5. 15 do	Rafting practice on Canal near WITTES.	
8. 5. 15 do	Received orders to move to WITTES next day to make room for a French Bridging Train. Sent billeting parties out. Rafting practice on canal near WITTES.	

WAR DIARY
INTELLIGENCE SUMMARY.
(Erase heading not required.)

Army Form C. 2118.

Instructions regarding War Diaries and Intelligence Summaries are contained in F. S. Regs., Part II, and the Staff Manual respectively. Title pages will be prepared in manuscript.

Hour, Date, Place.	Summary of Events and Information	Remarks and references to Appendices.
9. 5. 15 WITTES	Marched to WITTES in morning. Indispensables & kit etc sent billeted down in ideal billets – the best the Troop have had so far. The F. Squadron moved also to the same locality, sharing the buildings. Under 2 hours notice & expecting to move same night. Took ½ to sort & reduce kits.	
10. 5. 15 do	Under 2 hours notice. Kit reduced to summer scale.	
11. 5. 15 do	Under 2 hours notice. Got rid of doubtful explosives at the same time. Practising making up charges & firing.	
12. 5. 15 do	Under 2 hours notice. Sergt. Bawdrys transfers to G Squadron as Sq. Sergt. Major. L. Corp. Purcell transfers from Squadron in his place. Notice increased to 4 hours. 4 L.D. horses & 1 Riding horse arrived. Rafting practice on Lake.	
13. 5. 15 do	Heavy rain all day. No work. Suspected 2 H.D. horses.	
14. 5. 15 do	Experimenting with boat packing. Route march. Trying new L.D. horses.	
15. 5. 15 do	Rafting practice on Canal & laying charges for demolishing culverts electrically.	

WAR DIARY or INTELLIGENCE SUMMARY

Army Form C. 2118.

(Erase heading not required.)

Instructions regarding War Diaries and Intelligence Summaries are contained in F.S. Regs., Part II, and the Staff Manual respectively. Title pages will be prepared in manuscript.

p. 33

Hour, Date, Place.	Summary of Events and Information	Remarks and references to Appendices.
16. 5. 15 WITTES	Under 2 hours notice (Aeroscopt push near La Basseé developing) Sunday holiday. Encamped in Scalier farm.	
17. 5. 15 ALLOUAGNE	At 2 p.m. received orders to move same afternoon with Division + Field Squadron remaining behind to equip a train. Left at 4.20 p.m. & arrived ALLOUAGNE 11 p.m. Bivouac down. Under 1 minute's notice.	
18. 5. 15 do	Under immediate notice. Making arrangements for rapid move without A Echelon, if necessary, without toolcart & G.S. wagon.	
19. 5. 15 WITTES	Rehearsed col. of route in Echelons before arranging + packets for rapid move. Before the troop hd. demobilising orders was received to return to former billets same afternoon. Left with Division at 3.60 p.m. + arrived WITTES at 7.20 p.m. Evacuated farm. No one H.D. now suffering from "shivers". 6 ors new draught horses arrived.	
20. 5. 15 do	Assembling + fitting new harness. Painting linges + repairing tents. Under 4 hours notice. Can of tetanus Scalier farm Bivouaced.	
21. 5. 15 do	Inspection of all harness in horses. Painting linges.	
22. 5. 15 do	Fatigue Inspection made at 10 a.m.	

Army Form C. 2118.

WAR DIARY

INTELLIGENCE SUMMARY.

(Erase heading not required.)

Instructions regarding War Diaries and Intelligence Summaries are contained in F. S. Regs., Part II, and the Staff Manual respectively. Title pages will be prepared in manuscript.

Hour, Date, Place.	Summary of Events and Information	Remarks and references to Appendices.
WITTES		
22 - 5 - 15.	Painting linges; mending roof. SM/C 1 Indian Army (Jemamo) at RWHR.	
23 - 5 - 15.	do. Capt. Mann left on 7 days leave.	
24 - 5 - 15.	Holiday.	
25 - 5 - 15.	Practice mobilization parade in échelons — standing by to move to other billets to make room for British Cavalry returning from the trenches. Wagon repairs etc.	OC
26 - 5 - 15.	Physical training; swimming parade. Orders recd. towards evening for move of Division next day. JCJ.	
27 - 5 - 15. 10.45am. WITTES 1.15pm. STAPLE	Marched with division, leaving billets at 10.45 a.m. via BLARINGHEM — LYNDE — WALLONCAPPEL, arriving at STAPLE 1.15 p.m. At 11 p.m. of previous night, Sergt Gillett R.E. evacuated to hospital. The troop now has no R.E. NCO's. Dull day with wind, v. dusty; OC. previous week v. hot summer weather.	

Army Form C. 2118.

WAR DIARY
or
~~INTELLIGENCE SUMMARY.~~

(Erase heading not required.)

Instructions regarding War Diaries and Intelligence Summaries are contained in F. S. Regs., Part II, and the Staff Manual respectively. Title pages will be prepared in manuscript.

Hour, Date, Place.	Summary of Events and Information.	Remarks and references to Appendices
STAPLE 28-5-15 RUBROUCK 5pm	Marched to RUBROUCK, 10 a.m. to 12.30 p.m. — respirator drill 5pm orders received to join Division, which had marched	
near YPRES	(less Divl. Troops) to the neighbourhood of S.W. of VLAMERTINGHE. Orders as to route were received at 6.45 p.m. & unit marched out at 7.15pm via WORMHOUT — HERZEELE — WATOU — POPERINGHE	
near VLAMERTINGHE H 13 d 29-5-15	to H 13 d near VLAMERTINGHE when it arrived at 3.30 A.M. and bivouacked. Capt CHASE R.E. from 1st Ind. Fd. Squadron, attached in lieu of Capt Moring on leave, visited C.R.E. of 28th Div., who was to inspect his portion of trenches after dark — obtained leave from Divl. HQ. to accompany him. Inspected the line from wood S.W. of HOOGE northwards across MENIN road, due East of YPRES. One bicycle stolen during our absence — returned through YPRES, a desolate ruin, parts of which were still burning. At A.M. WARWICK. R.A.M.C. attached for duty from Fd Squadron).	× Capt Chase itself.
30-5-15 H 13 d	Men route marched — reconnoitred R.E. Park to ascertain information as regards supply of stores, & quantities required. Capt Chase visited line held by 3rd Cav. Div.	ACJ

Army Form C. 2118.

WAR DIARY
or
INTELLIGENCE SUMMARY.
(Erase heading not required.)

Instructions regarding War Diaries and Intelligence Summaries are contained in F. S. Regs., Part II, and the Staff Manual respectively. Title pages will be prepared in manuscript.

Hour, Date, Place.	Summary of Events and Information.	Remarks and references to Appendices
31. 5. near VLAMERTINGHE	Capt. Morris rejoined from leave. Received orders to go into Winter same night to help R.E. Coy. to put up Chevaux of Frise on MENIN Rd. wire state of Defence. Tho' several hitches & delays arrived too late to do any work. It appeared the Hun very busy night work & arrival back in camp at 6-am 1st June.	[signature] Capt 1/A OC Field Coy 3.6.18

WAR DIARY
OF

Field Troop, 1st Indian Cavalry Division

From 1st June 1915. To 30th June 1915.

Army Form C. 2118.

WAR DIARY
or
INTELLIGENCE SUMMARY.
(Erase heading not required.)

Instructions regarding War Diaries and Intelligence Summaries are contained in F.S. Regs., Part II, and the Staff Manual respectively. Title pages will be prepared in manuscript.

Hour, Date, Place.	Summary of Events and Information.	Remarks and references to Appendices.
1.6.15 VLAMERTINGHE	Moved at night to St Jean Chateau held by the K.D.G. Putting barbed wire round Chateau, making a strong point, digging communication lines from S.S.G.1 to "Dance" & making trench just below St Jean. Improvements to Jean billets. 6 wds in upper storeys. 3 men + 2 horses wounded. Mr Jasper wounded.	App. 1/6
2.6.15 Do	To Jean again at night. St Jean now heavily shelled during day & our trip was against work in the wood below fire lines as it was under fire. Had a comfortable trip in tops were enough to avoid Recipients in wood + eventually those 6 were then up. Chateau in the open and from 5p. Heavy to see from it as getting late. Left about 11.30pm & taken to New line Cad. William on left in a dug-out by the avenue. Brushes casualties Cpl Shaw one wd. Lce-Cpl in Foss + 1 private 2 night.	App. 2/6
3.6.15 Do	Keep Chateau having been no bombardment the Pays were not this night. K.R.R. Cpl & Cav 1 had landed 2/Lieut Boyce on after trouble to trenches. Re Func around the job brought if over from the front line Apps one slightly wounded. Capt Shaw was in command.	App. 3/6

Army Form C. 2118.

P.38

WAR DIARY
or
INTELLIGENCE SUMMARY.
(Erase heading not required.)

Instructions regarding War Diaries and Intelligence Summaries are contained in F. S. Regs., Part II, and the Staff Manual respectively. Title pages will be prepared in manuscript.

Hour, Date, Place.	Summary of Events and Information.	Remarks and references to Appendices.
4.6.15 VLAMERTINGHE	No night ask. Capt. Moore took command of "B" Sqn. Lt. Eyre Eyneson having gone up.	App 1/6
5/6 to 10	No work to the trenches. Practising Rapid wiring & Squadron went to Longleman's Farm time & trench wiring Drill.	App 2/6
11.6.15 90	Troop lent to "C" Sqn & directed to make a wiring party near "Hyde Corner" behind Hooge. Remainder that night	App 3/6
12.6.15 2	with Jemadars, Sgt. Peters & sharpshooters. Worked all night on strong point Ranstepen wounded. Capt Allen(?) & Stephen Hargreaves was also wounded on his way back to the work, with wagons of materials.	App 4/6
13.6.15	When about to start to make to before reached down 6 more early next morning with 1st Car. Di.	App 5/6
14.6.15 HAZEBROUCK	Marched with Bde to a point about 2 m. NE of HAZEBROUCK (near LA KREULE) & billeted.	App 14/6
15.6.15 16.6.15 LA SABLONNIÈRE	Marched with Bde to LA SABLONNIÈRE 5 m NW of AIRE & bivouacked.	App 15/6

Army Form C. 2118.

P. 39

WAR DIARY
of
INTELLIGENCE SUMMARY.
(Erase heading not required.)

Instructions regarding War Diaries and Intelligence Summaries are contained in F. S. Regs., Part II, and the Staff Manual respectively. Title pages will be prepared in manuscript.

Hour, Date, Place.	Summary of Events and Information.	Remarks and references to Appendices.
16.6.15 to 28.6.15 LA SABLONNIÈRE	Employed in practising digging trenches of different kinds by day & by night, also in doing various jobs for D.H.Q. & C.H.Q. Horses 'Duke' 'Tommy' evacuated on 28th. Under orders to work with Lahore Div. movement orders awaited.	Acc 26/6
29.6.15 RUE DU POUCH	Troops marched independently to RUE DU POUCH (3½ mile N of VIEILLE CHAPELLE) via AIRE, ST VENANT, CALONNE, LESTREM & FOSSE + went into billets. Reported to O/C 21st Coy (32nd S. M.) + received instructions about helping them. Also met CRE LAHORE + received general instructions. He foreshadowed permanent attachment to Lahore Div.	Appx 30/6
30.6.15 do	Started work in trenches during night of 30.6-1.7 working in front of support trenches from "northwards from a point about ½ m. NE. of NEUVE CHAPELLE	Acc 1/7

Almong Capt RE
Comm'g Field Troop
1st Indian Cav Div.

Serial No. 8. 144.

12/6948

WAR DIARY
OF
2nd Field Troop, Sappers and Miners.

FROM 1st August 1915 TO 31st August 1915

Army Form C. 2118.

Field Troop 5th M

A.G's OFFICE AT THE BASE
No. 1525 W.D
3 – SEP. 1915
INDIAN SECTION

P.45

WAR DIARY
or
INTELLIGENCE SUMMARY.
(Erase heading not required.)

Instructions regarding War Diaries and Intelligence Summaries are contained in F. S. Regs., Part II, and the Staff Manual respectively. Title pages will be prepared in manuscript.

Hour, Date, Place.	Summary of Events and Information.	Remarks and references to Appendices.
1.8.15 BOUT DELVILLE	Changed billets. the Troop being located in 2 adjoining farms, the horse transport in a separate field & the pony transport in another. A very inconvenient arrangement, it is no better one feasible.	Appx 4/7
2 to 6.8.15 do	Day work on EUSTON R⁴. improvement and CHATEAU CRUMP & KILL'S REDOUBT & CURZON POST – improvements & additions, water supply, M.G. emplacements &c.	Appx 6/7
7.8.15 do	Sunday – Rest.	Appx 7/7
8–14.8.15 do	Continued & completed above work & took up improvement of HUN ST. – removing revetting & boring for slabs – and construction of special bomb-prop shelters along LA BASSÉE R⁴.	Appx 7/7
15.8.15	Sunday – Rest.	
16–21.8.15 do	Still engaged on HUN ST & LA BASSÉE R⁴ – bomb con- struction on Z.ʲ 2.ʲ One Sapper wounded on Z.ʲ	Appx 7/7 Appx 8

Army Form C. 2118.

Pub

WAR DIARY
INTELLIGENCE SUMMARY.
(Erase heading not required.)

Instructions regarding War Diaries and Intelligence Summaries are contained in F.S. Regs., Part II, and the Staff Manual respectively. Title pages will be prepared in manuscript.

Hour, Date, Place.	Summary of Events and Information.	Remarks and references to Appendices.
21 – 26.8.15 BOUT DEINVILLE	Working on HUN ST & LA BASSEE Rd. Communication. Received orders on 26th to move to LACOUTURE & take over work of 21st Coy, along with 20th Coy.	AG/20/8
27.8.15 LACOUTURE	Moved to outskirts of LACOUTURE (Rue de Foix) & took up work of 21st & 81? Coy with 20th Coy	AG/27/8
28 – 31.8.15 do	Completing Dugouts at LANSDOWNE POST & improving & completing PENNY-MORRIS POST.	AG/5

Almon Col.
Comg Field Coy R.E.
1.9.15

121/7286

WAR DIARY OF

Field Troop Sappers and Miners.

From 1st September 1915 TO 30th September 1915

Army Form C. 2118.

Page 44

WAR DIARY
or
INTELLIGENCE SUMMARY.
(Erase heading not required.)

Instructions regarding War Diaries and Intelligence Summaries are contained in F. S. Regs., Part II, and the Staff Manual respectively. Title pages will be prepared in manuscript.

Hour, Date, Place.	Summary of Events and Information.	Remarks and references to Appendices.
1.9.15 LACOUTURE	Improvement roads in to PENIN-MARAIS, LANSDOWNE & ST VAAST POSTS.	Per 2/Lt
2.9.15 to	do	Per 2/Lt
8.9.15	do	
8.9.15	Constructing bridge on R. LOISNE & diversion R.2 road LACOUTURE with culvert. Constructing M.G. emplacement. Josais. NEUVE CHAPELLE cemeteries Old & new, & ST VAAST cemetery. Improving water supply at 6 places in front. Renovating EUSTON POST. Preparing M.G. emplacements.	Per 10/Lt
9.9.15 to 17.9.15		
18.9.15 to	Continued as above. Buried right B 18-19 feet in a new pattern M.G. emplacement in front line. Rest day (Sunday.)	Per 25/Lt ?
19.9.15 to		
20.9.15	Continued work on EUSTON POST &c. Attacked by Transport (letts shells) & set on fire. Drain Brown, Miller, Wood & Henderson wounded, 5 horses killed & wounded, and kit burnt.	Per 21/Lt

Army Form C. 2118.

Page 45

WAR DIARY
or
INTELLIGENCE SUMMARY.

(Erase heading not required.)

Instructions regarding War Diaries and Intelligence Summaries are contained in F. S. Regs., Part II, and the Staff Manual respectively. Title pages will be prepared in manuscript.

Hour, Date, Place.	Summary of Events and Information.	Remarks and references to Appendices.
21.9.15 to 23.9.15 LACOUTURE	Continuing work on EUSTON POST & other MD jobs	A/C 24/9
24.9.15	Making preparations for big attack on 25th	A/C 24/9
25.9.15	Standing to all day from 6 am. No service not required. LACOUTURE sketched in morning	A/C 25/9
26.9.15	Standing to as before (packed & ready to move). Afternoon improved crossing Rd. LACOUTURE sketched	A/C 30/9
27.9.15 to 30.9.15 do.	Working on EUSTON POST and flank defences & PONT LOGY communication.	A/C 4/10

Demmy Cole
Com. Field Coy R.E.
2.10.15

Serial No. 144

Confidential

121/7601

Diary

of

------- Field Troop Sappers and Miners.

FROM 1st October 1915. TO 31st October 1915.

Army Form C. 2118.

WAR DIARY
or
INTELLIGENCE SUMMARY.

(Erase heading not required.)

Instructions regarding War Diaries and Intelligence Summaries are contained in F. S. Regs., Part II, and the Staff Manual respectively. Title pages will be prepared in manuscript.

C8/2/10/11/15

Hour, Date, Place.	Summary of Events and Information.	Remarks and references to Appendices.
1. 1.10.15 LACOUTURE	Working on EUSTON POST and flank defences of PORTUGAL Communication. Received orders to billet at BOUT DELVILLE & await instructions	NC/ 3/10
2. 1.10.15 do		B
3. 6-7.10.15 BOUT-DELVILLE	Moved to BOUT-DELVILLE in 3½ trains or with same work	
8-31.10.15 Do	Working on huts along LA BASSÉE Rd, making them habitable for the winter. Received orders re departure from France	C8/ 31/10

Amor Capt
Cmdg Field Coy RE
1.11.15

Serial No. 10/144

12/7780

[signature]
En route to Basra
21.12.15

Confidential

War Diary

of

Field Troops Sappers and Miners

FROM 1st November 1915 TO 30th November 1915

Army Form C. 2118.

5th Devons 15
WAR DIARY
or
INTELLIGENCE SUMMARY.

(Erase heading not required.)

Instructions regarding War Diaries and Intelligence Summaries are contained in F. S. Regs., Part II, and the Staff Manual respectively. Title pages will be prepared in manuscript.

CR.
287
9 DEC 1915

Hour, Date, Place.	Summary of Events and Information.	Remarks and references to Appendices.
1.11.15 BOIS DELVILLE	Continued work on holdings on LA BASSES Rd. Received return from leave, leaving FRANCE	
2.11.15	Capt. Irwin went on leave. Continued alone	
3.11.15 to 7.11.15 20	work + practically completed the 3 holdings near LORETTO Rd. junction. Recce made of road to HAM-EN-ARTOIS	8.11.15
8.11.15 HAM-EN-ARTOIS	Capt. Irwin returned from leave. Moved to HAM-EN-ARTOIS in morning. Drew in motor lorries + billeted near Ry. station.	9.11.15
9.11.15 20	Settling down + resting	10.11.15
10.11.15 20	Rest + roads	10.11.15

For November
WAR DIARY

INTELLIGENCE SUMMARY.

(Erase heading not required.)

Army Form C. 2118.

Instructions regarding War Diaries and Intelligence Summaries are contained in F. S. Regs., Part II, and the Staff Manual respectively. Title pages will be prepared in manuscript.

Hour, Date, Place.	Summary of Events and Information.	Remarks and references to Appendices.
11 & 17. 11. 15 HAM-EN-ARTOIS	Resting; route marching, drilling, overhauling kit & equipt. Went eliminating, repairing. Renewing equipment. Changed horses for mules.	See 18 min
18. 11. 15 MAMETZ	Marched with Ferozepore Brigade to MAMETZ, 8 miles W. of AIRE, and bilettted down.	See 18 min
19. 11. 15 to 28. 11. 15 do	Resting - Ferozepore - route marching re. On 25th detachment from each unit, were told at NORRENT FONTES when H.H. The Prince of Wales read out a message from the King Emperor to the Indian Corps. An Indian was no heard from 21st to 28th.	See 28 min See 29 min
29. 11. 15 SENLIS	Marched with 20th & 21st Corps S.H. to SENLIS in pouring rain, very poor accommodation, much discomfort.	See 29 min
30. 11. 15 do	Settling down - tonight received orders to move to FEBVIN next day.	See 30 min Running case. Court Martial proc.

www.ingramcontent.com/pod-product-compliance
Lightning Source LLC
Chambersburg PA
CBHW081243170426
43191CB00034B/2019